MW01181252

# SWEET NOTHING IN MY EAR

A Play in Two Acts
by
STEPHEN SACHS

**Dramatic Publishing**
Woodstock, Illinois • London, England • Melbourne, Australia

IMPORTANT BILLING AND CREDIT REQUIREMENTS

All producers of the play *must* give credit to the author(s) of the play in all programs distributed in connection with performances of the play and in all instances in which the title of the play appears for purposes of advertising, publicizing or otherwise exploiting the play and/or a production. The name of the author(s) *must* also appear on a separate line, on which no other name appears, immediately following the title, and *must* appear in size of type not less than fifty percent the size of the title type. Biographical information on the author(s), if included in this book, may be used on all programs. *On all programs this notice must appear:*

## The Language of the Play

This is not a "deaf" play. It's a play with deaf and hearing characters.

In performance, it must be accessible to both a deaf and hearing audience at the same time. It requires a seamless blend of American Sign Language and spoken English. The two languages happen simultaneously throughout the performance of the play.

The role of Dan requires a hearing actor who signs well. As a hearing man in a deaf family, he is called upon to interpret speech into sign language, "voice" ASL into speech, or switch his voice off completely and purely sign. Whenever Dan is alone with any member of his deaf family, he would only sign and not use his voice (unless indicated).

All the deaf characters of the play—Laura, Max, Sally, Adam, Dr. Walters—use only American Sign Language. They are simultaneously "voiced" or "voice acted" from the side of the stage by a member of the Company. When Dan switches off his voice and purely signs, he is simultaneously "voiced" by a Company member.

The Company must be four hearing actors who sign. They sit on the periphery of the stage, never leaving, throughout the play. They perform three functions: to "voice" the actors who sign, to sign the actors who speak, and to step forward as the supporting players.

Deaf audience members experience this play signed entirely in their language. Hearing audience members—most who know nothing of sign language—have the experience of watching the play in sign language while hearing it acted at the same time.

Two languages become one.

— Stephen Sachs

*SWEET NOTHING IN MY EAR* was originally produced by Deborah Lawlor and Jesica Korbman for The Fountain Theatre in Los Angeles, June 1997. It was directed by Stephen Sachs, set design by Sets to Go; costume design by Mariel McEwan; lighting design by J. Kent Inasy; slide projections were created by Evan Mower; and the production stage manager was Jesica Korbman. The cast was as follows:

Dan ....................................... BOB KIRSH
Laura .................................... TERRYLENE
Adam ........................... GIANNI MANGANELLI
Voice of Laura / Pam Scott ............ JENNIFER MASSEY
Dr. Weisman / Voice of Dan ................ JOHN BENITZ
Barbara Cannon / Voices of Sally, Adam, Dr. Walters ........
......................................... ELIZABETH BARRETT
Max ............................... BERNARD BRAGG
Voice of Max / Dr. Flynt ................. CAL BARTLETT
Sally ................................ FREDA NORMAN
Dr. Walters ........................... VIKEE WALTRIP

*SWEET NOTHING IN MY EAR* was produced at the Victory Gardens Theater in Chicago by Simon Levy for The Fountain Theatre and M.T. Productions, March 1998. It was directed by Stephen Sachs; set design by Sets to Go; costume design by Kristine Knanishu; lighting design by Joel Moritz; sound design by Lindsay Jones; slide projections were created by Evan Mower; and the production stage manager was Meredith Scott Brittain. The cast was as follows:

Dan .................................... PHILIP LESTER
Laura ........................ LIZ TANNEBAUM-GRECO
Adam .................... GEORGE SCOTT KARTHEISER
Voice of Laura / Pam Scott ............ JENNIFER MASSEY
Dr. Weisman / Voice of Dan ................ JOHN BENITZ
Barbara Cannon / Voices of Sally, Adam, Dr. Walters ........
......................................... ELIZABETH BARRETT
Max ................................. CHUCK BAIRD
Voice of Max / Dr. Flynt ................. CAL BARTLETT
Sally ................................ VIKEE WALTRIP
Dr. Walters ................................. RALITSA

# SWEET NOTHING IN MY EAR

A Play in Two Acts
For 4 Men, 5 Women and 1 boy

## CHARACTERS

LAURA ........................ a deaf school teacher
DAN ........................... her hearing husband
ADAM ..................... their deaf six year-old son
MAX .......................... deaf, Laura's father
SALLY ....................... deaf, Laura's mother
DR. WALTERS ..................... a deaf therapist

THE COMPANY (hearing actors who sign) assume the
following roles:

DR. WEISMAN (and "voice" of Dan)
BARBARA CANNON (and "voice" of Sally, Adam,
                                    Dr. Walters)
DR. FLYNT (and "voice" of Max)
PAMELA SCOTT (and "voice" of Laura)

Approximate running time: 1 hour, 50 minutes.

One unit set, various locations.

# ACT ONE

SETTING: *A bare stage. One table and a collection of chairs become the various locations of the play. The up-stage walls around the playing area are equipped for rear-screen slide projection.*

AT RISE: *LIGHTS DIM. The COMPANY enters and takes their place around the playing area. They remain on-stage throughout the play, stepping in as characters and "voicing" for deaf actors. They sit. BLACKOUT.*

*Classroom. A single SPOTLIGHT on LAURA. In a graceful flow of American Sign Language, she signs a children's story to an unseen classroom of kids sitting in front of her on the floor.*

LAURA. Okay, kids look at me! *(Her hands circling.)* Once upon a time, there was a little bird who couldn't fly.

*(SLIDE PROJECTION: A child's colorful crayon draw-ing of a bird.)*

He would watch all the other birds spread their wings and rise above the trees and soar through the clouds. One day, the little bird asked his mother, "Why can't I

7

fly like the other birds?" "But, *I* can't fly either. And neither can your brothers and sisters, your aunts, your uncles. All the people who love you." "Doesn't it bother you that you can't fly?" asked the little bird. "There's much more to being a bird than flying. And if I could fly, it wouldn't make me love you any more than I do now." But the little bird didn't understand.

*(SLIDE PROJECTION: A child's crayon drawing of a snake.)*

One night, a big snake, shining with every color of the rainbow, appeared before the little bird. "I am a magic snake. I will grant you any wish in all the world. What do you wish for?" "That's easy!" said the little bird. "I want to fly like the other birds!" "Beware!" said the snake. "If I give your wings the ability to fly, you will no longer be the same as your family on the ground. They are happy and love you as you are. You must choose where you belong. What is your wish?"

*(SPOTLIGHT on DAN, sitting, facing front. A COURT INTERPRETER stands beside him, translating the following into ASL as DAN speaks.)*

DAN. They say a baby can hear inside the womb. So, all through Laura's pregnancy, I put my mouth close to her belly and spoke to Adam inside her. "Hello, Adam... How's it going in there?... I love you... I can't wait to see you..." I talked to him like that for months, all the time imagining him floating inside Laura, bathed by the sound of my voice. Laura would tease me: "What if he can't hear you?" I'd laugh and press my hand against her belly and sign to Adam *(demonstrates)*, "I love you," just in case. I was in the delivery room on the day that he was born. He was crying and crying when they handed him to me, but when I spoke to him: "Ssshhh, Adam... It's okay... it's me, Daddy..." He stopped crying, opened his eyes, and looked up at me. It was the sound of my voice—he recognized it—like we knew each other already. *(A question.)* Uh, it started when Adam was six. More than a year ago. At that time I worked out of my home. That was my choice. To be closer to Adam.

*(SLIDE PROJECTION: A child's crayon drawing of a doctor's office.)*

*(Lights up on doctor's office. ADAM sits on the examination table. Blood runs from his knee. DR. WEISMAN examines the wound as DAN hovers beside them. As he speaks, DAN interprets everything into ASL for ADAM until indicated.)*

DAN *(continuing; upset, speaking and signing)*. He was running across the backyard chasing a balloon, not looking where he was going. I could see he was going to trip over the bike. I couldn't get to him! I yelled out—reflex, like he's still hearing—"Adam! Stop! Look out!" But he couldn't hear me! I had to watch him fall and hurt himself.

DR. WEISMAN. It's a nasty cut.

DAN. The parents' nightmare, right? Your kid's about to get hurt. You scream out but can't stop him.

DR. WEISMAN. Kids fall all the time.

DAN *(agitated)*. But with other kids when you scream out, they stop. I mean— *(Looks to ADAM.)* Never mind.

ADAM *(signing to DOCTOR)*. "It's my birthday!"

DAN. His birthday party's tomorrow.

DR. WEISMAN *(speaking to ADAM)*. Oh. Well. Happy birthday. And if you could have any present for your birthday, what would it be?

ADAM *(DAN voices)*. "Power Rangers video game for my computer!"

DR. WEISMAN *(about to apply solvent to knee)*. Tell him this might sting a bit.

DAN *(signing to ADAM)*. That might sting a little. *(Trying to distract him.)* Wow! Look at all this new computer equipment! Very cool, huh? *(To DOCTOR.)* Was this all here before?

DR. WEISMAN. No. I brought it in. After Dr. Peters left. *(He dabs the wound.)*

ADAM *(crying out, pulling his leg away)*. Oooowwwwww!

DAN *(soothing him)*. I know, I know, he just wants to clean it. That's all. Will you let him do that? Okay? *(ADAM reluctantly offers his knee back to DR. WEISMAN who dabs the wound again.)*

ADAM. ooooowwwwwwwwwww!

DR. WEISMAN *(rises to get supplies)*. He's going to need a stitch or two.

DAN. Really?

DR. WEISMAN. Can you hold his leg for me with both hands?

DAN. If I hold his leg with both hands I can't sign to him.

DR. WEISMAN. Of course. *(Into intercom.)* Janet, when you finish in room two can you help me in one, please?

DAN *(anxious, speaking to himself).* Oh, God. *(Speaking and signing to ADAM.)* Remember when your bear got ripped, and Mommy sewed him back up? Made him better? *(ADAM nods.)* Well, that's what the doctor's going to do to the boo-boo on your knee! Stitch it up! Just like your bear!

ADAM. Will it hurt?

*(DAN looks to DOCTOR.)*

DR. WEISMAN *(to ADAM, DAN interprets).* Not a bit! I'll put some special medicine on it first, you won't feel a thing! *(To DAN.)* The nurse will be right in. It won't take long.

DAN *(to ADAM).* This is a lousy way to meet the new doctor, isn't it?

DR. WEISMAN *(reviewing ADAM's chart).* When did Adam begin to lose his hearing?

DAN. About two years ago.

DR. WEISMAN. He doesn't wear hearing aids?

DAN. They stopped helping.

DR. WEISMAN. And now, at six, he's at total hearing loss.

DAN. All this is in his file.

DR. WEISMAN. It must have required quite an adjustment.

DAN. His deafness isn't a problem, I've accepted it.

DR. WEISMAN. I meant for him.

DAN. Adam's been signing since he was a little—his Mother is deaf. In fact, his first word was signed, not spoken. Even though he was born hearing. *(To ADAM.)* Mommy taught you to sign, right?

ADAM *(DAN voicing ADAM)*. "Mommy—give—me—magic—hands."

DAN *(to DOCTOR)*. She tells him his hands are magic because "they speak all the words in the world, express all the colors of the rainbow, and are as beautiful as the stars." *(To ADAM.)* Right?

*(ADAM signs back, "Right!")*

DR. WEISMAN. How's his speech?

DAN. He doesn't speak. Anymore. We used to talk all the time. But he seems to have stopped. Speaking. To me. *(Anxious.)* Maybe I should call Laura. She's at work. She teaches deaf children.

DR. WEISMAN. When did he stop speaking?

DAN. Six months ago. May 11th. To be exact.

DR. WEISMAN *(writing note in folder)*. May 11th?

DAN. Mother's Day. He just— *(He makes a hand gesture of turning a switch at his throat.)*

DR. WEISMAN. What's that?

DAN. It means he "turned off his voice."

DR. WEISMAN. He might turn it back on if he could hear himself speak.

DAN. We can't reverse what God does, right?

DR. WEISMAN. Sometimes we can. Have you ever heard of a cochlear implant?

*(DAN starts to interpret this last remark for ADAM. Stops. Drops his hands. DAN now speaks only, He does not interpret any of it for ADAM. [Note: The following is interpreted for the audience into sign language by the company.])*

DR. WEISMAN. Have you and your wife ever considered one for Adam?

DAN. No. Of course not.

DR. WEISMAN. He's an excellent candidate for one. Even Dr. Peters thought so.

DAN. He did not.

DR. WEISMAN. He wrote it in his notes. Over a year ago. *(Holding up paper.)* I can show you.

*(DAN waves the paper away.)*

He never said anything to you or your wife?

DAN. He knew we'd never agree to that.

DR. WEISMAN. Do you know how an implant works?

DAN. We don't want anything stuck in his head.

ADAM *(signs anxiously to DAN, voiced by DAN)*. Will it hurt? Don't let him hurt me!

DAN *(confused, signing and speaking to ADAM)*. What?... No! Don't worry! I won't let anybody hurt you! *(To DOCTOR.)* Shouldn't the nurse be here by now?

DR. WEISMAN. A hearing aid only amplifies sound. An implant has a tiny computer chip that translates the sound into an electronic code that is sent directly to the brain. The technology is now so advanced—the implants are small, virtually undetectable.

DAN. He doesn't need a computer in his brain! He's not a robot!

DR. WEISMAN. The child hears sound again.

DAN. Not fully. Not like a hearing child.

DR. WEISMAN. Some hearing is better than no hearing. Right? *(DAN does not respond.)* As an implant candidate, Adam has two advantages. He lost his hearing after already learning oral speech. And he has four years of hearing memory. So the concept of sound and speech is not foreign to him.

DAN. He also has a deaf mother, deaf grandparents, an entire side of his family is deaf. There's a huge deaf community out there.

DR. WEISMAN. If his heart were defective you wouldn't question implanting an artificial valve.

DAN. The deaf don't see themselves as defective. That's the point.

DR. WEISMAN. Well, from a medical standpoint—

DAN. I've been married to a deaf woman for seven years. Nothing about her is defective.

DR. WEISMAN. I don't mean to insult anyone.

DAN. Laura's deafness is not an issue with me. And Adam's deafness is not a problem that needs correcting. I want you to fix his knee! Not his brain!

DR. WEISMAN. All I'm saying is you and your wife are lucky. Technology is giving you the opportunity to choose.

DAN. Choose what?

DR. WEISMAN. Whether Adam should be hearing or deaf.

DAN. That choice has been made.

DR. WEISMAN. The longer he remains deaf, the less effective an implant would be in recovering his hearing. So time is a factor. Here... *(Writing on pad.)* Call Dr. Flynt at the Hearing Institute downtown. He can help you. But, remember, you're running out of time. *(He holds out the slip of paper. DAN does not take it.)*

DAN. The deaf have a sign for those implants. Do you know what it is? It's this. *(Demonstrates, curving his first two fingers and stabbing them into the side of his neck.)* It's the same sign for "vampire." Something evil that drains the life out of you.

DR. WEISMAN *(still holding out slip of paper).* Take it. It's not an evil monster. It's only information. Information can't hurt you.

*(SPOTLIGHT on BARBARA CANNON, sitting, facing front. A COURT INTERPRETER stands beside her, translating into ASL.)*

BARBARA CANNON *(speaking).* For the record, my name is— *(Fingerspelling.)* B-a-r-b-a-r-a C-a-n-n-o-n. I have a Ph.D. in linguistics and teach American Sign Language at the Woodward School for the Deaf. *(A question.)* Well, first, it's important to understand that American Sign Language is not a mimed approximation of spoken English. It is an entirely unique, complex language unto itself. It has its own vocabulary, syntax, grammar, sentence structure, slang. It even has its own regional dialects. And, of course, Sign differs from country to country. There is British Sign Language, Russian Sign Language, Chinese Sign Language. *(A question.)* Well, maybe the single most remarkable aspect of Sign—what sets it apart from all other languages—is that it is the only language in the world that is four-dimensional. Speech has only one dimension. Writing has two. But only Sign is communicated through the three dimensions of the human body with the added dimension of time in space. The complexity of Sign is astonishing and completely inconceivable to the untrained eye. It may appear simple, like gesture or pantomime. But the limitless number of spacial relationships of the hands in four dimensions make Sign a language of overwhelming intricacy, subtlety and beauty. And it is more than that. It is impossible for a hearing person to fully comprehend the power Sign gives to the deaf. It is the electric current through which surges their thought, their soul, their history, their culture. If that electric plug were ever pulled...

*(SLIDE PROJECTION: A child's crayon drawing of his birthday party in his backyard.)*

*(LIGHTS UP on the backyard. A table with unwrapped birthday gifts is upstage. ADAM sits playing with a pocket computer game. He has a bandage on his knee. DAN watches him, deep in thought. LAURA briskly enters from the house. MAX follows. DAN signs only with the family and does not speak.)*

LAURA *(rapidly)*. Where do fifteen kids get all that energy? Everything is run, run, run! Of course, give fifteen kids chocolate birthday cake and ice cream and what do you expect? They shoot off into space like rockets! *(She laughs.)* An article came out in the newspaper. A recent study by a panel of experts had determined that sugar did not have an affect on children. Of course sugar makes kids bonkers! I'd like to hire a panel to find out some IMPORTANT questions, like: why is there always one kid's sock missing when you pull the laundry out of the dryer? Never a pair, always *one* sock! It was there when you put the laundry in, now it's gone! WHERE does it go? Nobody knows! *(A pause.)*

MAX. How much cake have you had?

LAURA *(laughs, gets DAN's attention)*. You're not paying attention.

DAN. I am.

LAURA. Your eyes keep going to Adam.

DAN. I'm just...thinking about his knee. That's all.

LAURA *(kissing DAN)*. You act as if YOU fell down, not him. *(To MAX.)* Where's Mom?

MAX. In the kitchen. Washing plates.

LAURA. They're paper plates! We throw them away! She doesn't need to wash them!

MAX. Cleaning makes her happy.

LAURA. Cleaning makes NOBODY happy!

MAX. *(not moving)*. She's fine.

LAURA. You know that TV show, *Unsolved Mysteries*? *(MAX nods. She smiles.)* They should try to find out why Mom has stayed married to you all these years.

*(She exits into the house. DAN and MAX are alone with ADAM. There is an uncomfortable silence between them. DAN crosses to ADAM.)*

DAN *(kissing ADAM's head)*. Did you like your birthday party? It was great seeing all your friends here!

ADAM. But Mark didn't come! Why?

DAN *(uncomfortable)*. His mommy called...she said he didn't feel well.

ADAM. He doesn't like me anymore.

DAN. Sure he does! He still likes you!

ADAM. He said I was weird now—

MAX *(interrupting)*. Who said that? Who's Mark?

DAN. The boy next door.

MAX. The hearing boy.

DAN *(tense)*. Yes, the hearing boy next door.

MAX *(to ADAM)*. Don't worry about Mark. Forget about him!

DAN *(sharp, to MAX)*. I'll handle this, okay?

*(MAX crosses away to the table.)*

You're a wonderful boy. Don't you ever forget that. You're the most important thing in the world to me. *(Hugs his son tight.)* As you grow up, you're going to have many, many friends—some deaf, some hearing.

ADAM. Do *you* have hearing friends?

DAN. ME? *(Chuckles.)* Yes, of course. I have a lot— *(Stops. Thinks. Realizes.)* Well, I mean ... Now that I think about it ... I used to ... *(A pause.)* How's your knee? Does it still hurt?

ADAM. Nope! I have a Band-aid!

*(At the table, MAX gets the attention of DAN. Picks up the small pack of baseball cards.)*

MAX. I drove all over the city to find these baseball cards for him. Three different shops. I explained each time—I even wrote it down—"Very important." "For grandson." "Must be Dodgers." "Must be whole starting lineup." *(He looks at ADAM.)* When he opened them, he looked confused. Like he didn't know what they were. You never gave him baseball cards before?

DAN. He's got computer baseball cards now. All on CD-ROM. He clicks the mouse and gets his favorite player, a

million stats, and full-color highlights of each player's
career.

MAX. Do they put a stick of bubble gum in the disk?

DAN. I don't think so.

MAX. He's only six.

DAN. He caught my computer bug.

MAX. You infected him.

DAN. They put a computer in his classroom when he was
three.

MAX. The hearing school did that.

DAN. Yes, the hearing school did that! That's not the
point!

MAX. What *is* the point?

DAN. Adam is not deaf in cyberspace. Technology is the
Great Equalizer. That's the beauty of it. Hearing is not
an issue on the Internet. It's all just pure data. Pure information. Pure communication.

MAX. ASL is pure communication. It's visual. It's alive.
You can't type it on a keyboard. It needs two living,
breathing human beings, facing each other. Interacting.
Sign language would evaporate in cyberspace.

DAN. They now have a computer that reads ASL! Yes!
You sign into the monitor, the computer reads your signs
with a visual sensor and translates it into digital signals—

MAX. It's not the same thing. I don't want my grandson to
grow up, look back on his childhood, and realize that his
best friend was a monitor!

*(LAURA enters from the house with SALLY, wiping her
hands with a dish towel. SALLY has a flower painted on
her cheek.)*

SALLY. That was a wonderful birthday party! I love seeing a backyard full of happy little deaf children! Running! Laughing! Playing!

LAURA *(laughing)*. What about *you*? Running around with
all those kids! Why did we pay $150 for a guy dressed
like Batman when we have you?

SALLY. Did I make a fool of myself?

MAX *(starting to say "yes")*. Well—

LAURA *(interrupting, to SALLY)*. No, it's great.

MAX. I think you dancing around the backyard pretending
you're a chicken is carrying things too far. If you ask
me.

LAURA. Nobody asked you.

SALLY. I wasn't a chicken! I was a goose! Mother Goose!

MAX. You've got paint on your face.

SALLY *(wiping her cheek)*. Oh! Sorry!

MAX. What is that? A cow?

SALLY *(rubbing cheek harder)*. No. It's a flower. Batman
was painting the children's faces. He asked me what I
wanted on my face. I said, a flower.

LAURA *(holding the dish towel out to ADAM)*. Can you
help clean it?

*(As ADAM and LAURA wipe flower from SALLY's face:)*

SALLY *(to LAURA)*. You're lucky to work with kids every
day.

LAURA. Oh, there's this girl in my class. She was very
sad. I asked her what's wrong. She said, "When I go
home I can't talk to my mommy because she's hearing
and doesn't know sign language." So, I explained to the
mother what her daughter was feeling. Well, the mother,

without telling her daughter, began sign language class. Secretly, to surprise her daughter. On Sunday, she took her to church. In the middle of the service, the mother signed the Lord's Prayer with her daughter, for the first time! Well, the girl comes running into class the next morning: "Guess what? It's a miracle! God cured my mommy's hearing! Now, she's deaf!" *(They laugh. LAURA crosses to ADAM.)* Hey, didn't you let Batman paint *your* face?

ADAM. No.

LAURA. Why not? You're the birthday boy!

*(ADAM pulls up his shirt. On his tummy is painted a huge, brightly colored birthday cake with six candles.)*

*(Delighted.)* Oh! Wow! How many candles on your birthday cake? Six? I better blow them out!

*(She presses her mouth on his tummy and blows hard. ADAM laughs and giggles! DAN crosses to them and picks ADAM up from LAURA.)*

DAN. Okay, birthday boy, let's go inside and check out some of your new computer games! Yay!

*(They start to exit. MAX stops them.)*

MAX *(to ADAM)*. Wait! Come here. *(Pulls ADAM away from DAN.)* What's your favorite baseball team?

ADAM. Dodgers.

MAX. Good. See? *(Showing ADAM baseball cards.)* All Dodgers! Did you know there once was an outfielder for the Cincinnati Reds who threw out three runners at home plate in one game, setting a new record? And he stole so many bases that he's on the top twenty list of all time? And you know what else was special about him? He was deaf! That's right! He only had one problem: he couldn't hear the umpire call out balls or strikes. So you know what they did? They started using hand signals—sign language—to show the count. Like this. *(Demonstrating.)* "Three and two!" See? And they still do it to this day!

DAN *(crossing to ADAM)*. And when the player strikes out, the umpire always yells real loud, "Yooou'rree OOOOOUUUT!" *(Moving closer to ADAM.)* Can you do that? Use your voice! Big and loud! "YOOOOOU'RRRE OOOOOOUUUUUT!" Come on, use your voice, you can do it. "YOOOOOOOOU'RE OOOOUUUT!"

MAX *(getting ADAM's attention)*. There was a deaf pitcher for the New York Giants. Pitched nineteen years, including in the World Series! Did you know that?

ADAM *(turns to his mother)*. Can I play with my computer now?

LAURA. Sure. Go ahead.

*(ADAM exits. There is an uncomfortable silence between the adults.)*

*(To DAN.)* His knee is better today.

SALLY. Dr. Peters is wonderful.
LAURA. Dr. Peters retired.
DAN. He has a new doctor now. He's very good.
MAX. Is he hearing or deaf?

DAN. He's hearing! What does that have to do with—

SALLY *(interrupting, to LAURA).* I remember when I brought you in to see Dr. Peters. Just a few days after you were born.

LAURA. What was wrong with me?

SALLY. Nothing. He just wanted to count your fingers, count your toes. You were so tiny—so precious. I held you in my arms for nine days and never put you down. I'd feed you. Change you. Watch you sleep in my arms. Praying to God to give me strength.

LAURA. Strength for what?

SALLY. To follow His will.

DAN. When God made Laura, He made no mistakes. *(DAN and LAURA kiss with true passion.)*

*(SLIDE PROJECTION: A child's crayon drawing of a night sky, with moon and stars.)*

*(Bedroom. LIGHTS UP on DAN and LAURA, kissing and embracing. They slowly undress each other and move to the bed. They begin making love. She places her hand within his palm and signs the hand shape "I Love You" [voiced by COMPANY member]. DAN feels her sign in his hand and puts his hand in her palm, returning the sign "I love you" [voiced by COMPANY member] and then adds the sign "forever" [spoken by COMPANY member]. DAN pulls away and sits up in bed, signing to LAURA.)*

DAN. Chasing a balloon. That's all he was doing. I yelled to him. Stop! Watch out! But he couldn't hear me. I had to watch him fall. And hurt himself. Like a nightmare.

LAURA. Why are you obsessing about that now? *(Teasing, sensually.)* Don't you like me anymore?

DAN. In my mind, he falls, and falls... and keeps falling.

LAURA *(flips a "switch" on the side of his head)*. Then turn your mind off. Like your computer.

DAN. Yes, computers in our heads.

LAURA. I saw you and Dad bickering today. You two are like children!

DAN. He's never truly accepted me. Not from the beginning.

LAURA. He accepts you.

DAN. He tolerates me. Barely.

LAURA. He comes from a hearing family—

DAN. —I know! I've heard the horror stories. Again and again!

LAURA. His parents rejected him. Sent him away. But Dad isn't prejudiced. Anymore. It's just his way. It's not because you're hearing—

DAN. Of course it is! Don't underestimate prejudice. It can lie dormant for years. Like a virus.

LAURA *(looks at him; hard)*. What's gotten into you? Something's happened.

DAN. Nothing's happened.

LAURA. Adam is all right.

DAN. Adam is not all right.

LAURA. He's going to trip and fall again. There's nothing we can do to prevent it.

DAN. Maybe there is. What if next time—I mean, God forbid it should ever happen—but, what if, next time, he's chasing the yellow balloon, and it leads him into traffic? He can't hear cars. He can't hear me yell stop.

LAURA. He never runs into the street without looking.

DAN. Never?

LAURA. Never.

DAN. How do you know?

LAURA. Because I TAUGHT him. Deaf kids don't just wander off into traffic. You know that. You never read about deaf kids walking aimlessly into traffic. It doesn't happen.

DAN. I just love him so much.

LAURA. I know. I love him too.

DAN. And I want him to live a full life.

LAURA. I'm living a full life.

DAN. I know, I want him to have every opportunity available to him.

LAURA. He's a very happy boy. Look at him, he loves life. He loves his family. Everything is as it should be.

DAN. Is it?

LAURA. Yes.

DAN. What if... we were given the ability, the power, to change the direction of his life...

LAURA *(confused)*. Like Mom said today, all you can do is clutch your baby tight and pray for guidance.

DAN. God has nothing to do with it! Things are different now. Computer microchips. Signal processors. Electronic receivers. These have the power to heal now. Not God! *(A pause.)* When I spoke to the new doctor, he said we have an option.

LAURA. What option?

DAN. That we have the... unique opportunity to choose whether Adam is... *(He stops.)* A cochlear implant—

LAURA *(recoiling)*. A COCHLEAR IMPLANT?

DAN. The doctor said Adam's a good candidate for one.

LAURA. No!

DAN. *If* we took that path—

LAURA. ABSOLUTELY NOT!

DAN. That's what I said!

LAURA. I don't want them drilling into Adam's skull and putting wires in his head. Why? What for?

DAN. That's exactly what I told him.

LAURA. Good.

DAN. Then he explained that it's not like that anymore. It's a new world now, technology has advanced, it's shooting us into another universe. These implants today are small, harmless and you can hardly see them. They have 24-channel sound and are powered by a computer microchip. *(She stares at him. He quickly pulls out the slip of paper.)* There's this doctor, Doctor Flynt. Apparently, he's got all the answers! *(He holds out the paper to her. She doesn't take it.)* Let's go see him. Just find out what our options are.

LAURA. Why?

DAN. Because WHAT IF? What if this tiny computer chip can make our boy hear again!

LAURA. I've heard of deaf people who had them. That boy who said it made him dizzy. That woman who got all those headaches. They took them out and threw them away!

DAN. But remember a few years ago on TV? We saw that boy who had one! He loved it!

LAURA. You and I turned that TV show off!

DAN. He could suddenly hear all those things! He was now going to public school, playing with hearing children—

LAURA. Deaf kids go to public schools and play with hearing children!

DAN. It changed his life! There are thousands like him out there!

LAURA. We thought that TV show was terrible!

DAN. We didn't have Adam then!

LAURA. He's a deaf child now! He's happy the way he is!

DAN. You mean *you're* happy the way he is.

LAURA. What does that mean?

DAN. You always wanted a deaf child. Now you've got one. *(They stare at each other.)* I don't know what I'm saying.

LAURA. Yes, you do.

DAN. I'm saying, what harm does it do to meet Dr. Flynt? Talk to him. How can we make an intelligent decision without having all the facts? For Adam's sake.

LAURA. This isn't about Adam.

DAN. Of course it is.

LAURA. Adam isn't asking for an implant.

DAN. He's only six! He doesn't even know they exist!

LAURA. Tell him! Ask him what he wants!

DAN. He's a child! He can't possibly understand!

LAURA. Let him grow up! As an adult, he can decide for himself!

DAN. There's a time factor here.

LAURA. What time factor?

DAN. The older he gets, the longer he's deaf, the less effective an implant will be. The doctor said he may now still remember what things sound like.

LAURA. I've taught Adam to love who he is. He's gone from being a hearing child who speaks to Daddy but signs to Mommy, to being a hard-of-hearing child with hearing aids who speaks to hearing people and signs at home, to becoming a totally deaf child! And now you want to pull the process back and stick something in his head so he can maybe hear again? Why?

DAN. To give back to him one of the basic, human senses that Nature wants all of us to have!

LAURA. It's obvious what Nature wants! Nature wants Adam to be deaf! Because that's what's happened! Nature did it! You're the one who wants to fuck with it! If we pull him back and forth too much he'll break!

DAN. All I want is for Adam to have the best shot at life that he can!

LAURA. A deaf person doesn't have a "best shot at life"? Everything he needs is already inside him! Intact!

DAN. You know what I mean!

LAURA. Adam and I have a language! A community! A family!

DAN. *I'm* his family, too! It's not just you and Adam in a secret club, and me on the outside—

LAURA. Is that how you feel?

DAN. Let's just meet with Dr. Flynt. On Friday.

LAURA. Friday?

DAN. Yes. At three forty-five. *(A pause.)*

LAURA. You already made an appointment.

DAN. Yes. *(She looks at him.)* There's a time factor here. These doctors are so busy. You have to catch them when you can. *(She stares at him.)* What?

LAURA. You've already made up your mind.

DAN. No, I'm keeping mine open. Can you?

*(SPOTLIGHT on MAX, sitting, facing front.)*

MAX *(answering a question).* What is Deaf Pride? It's something you're born with. If you're born deaf. *(An-*

*other question.)* No, I'm not saying you're more deaf if you're born deaf, but, yes, if you're born deaf you have a deeper understanding, a deeper appreciation, of what Deaf Pride is. That's what I taught my daughter. *(Another question.)* It was about a year ago, around Adam's sixth birthday. I was shocked. Stunned—when Laura first told me what Dan wanted to do. Barbaric. It made me think back to the days when hospitals would slice out the bottom of the tongues of deaf people—to "loosen their tongues"—thinking that would get them to speak like hearing people. *(Another question.)* No. I don't think Dan's a bad man. He's a hearing man. He thinks I'm a bigot. Prejudiced. I'm not. But, like most hearing people, he thought a deaf person, if given the chance, would rather be hearing than deaf. Most hearing people think that. If you were to say to a black man, "Take this magic pill. It will make you white and all the doors in the world will be open to you!" do you think he would take the pill? Of course not! He'd say "Fuck you!" Excuse me. He'd say, "No! I have my culture! I have my people! I have my identity! Leave me alone! Let me be!" The majority assumes that each minority wants to be like them. But, as my wife says, God made us all different for a reason.

*(SLIDE PROJECTION: A child's crayon drawing of a TV set with a caption decoder box on it.)*

*(Living room. ADAM sits, watching TV. LAURA approaches.)*

LAURA. What're you watching?

ADAM. Bambi.

LAURA. Oh, I can't watch that! I've seen it eight million times and it always makes me cry!

ADAM. Yeah. When Bambi's mother—

LAURA. Don't! Don't even sign it! *(He looks at her.)* Don't worry. I'm not going anywhere. You're stuck with me.

ADAM *(pointing to TV)*. How do they do that?

LAURA. Do what?

ADAM. Put words in.

LAURA. Captions? Well, the TV signal flies through the air. And, uh, goes into the ... at the same time the ... the truth is, I have no idea how they do that.

ADAM. Is it magic?

LAURA. No, it's not magic. It's ... technology.

ADAM. Computers?

LAURA. Yes. Computers put words on the bottom of the screen so we know what the animals are saying.

ADAM. Computers are good.

LAURA. Sometimes. *(They watch TV.)* Do you remember sound?

ADAM. Some things.

LAURA. What things? *(He doesn't answer.)* It's okay. Do you remember when you used to watch TV with the sound on so loud? It made Daddy crazy.

ADAM. Made me crazy, too.

LAURA. But things are better now, right? You're happy now, right?

ADAM. No.

LAURA. No? Why aren't you happy?

ADAM. I don't want to be Happy. I want to be Doc. You be Dopey. Daddy will be Sleepy. Nana can be Grumpy—

LAURA *(laughing with relief)*. Oh! I get it!

ADAM. Do you remember sound?

LAURA. Me? No. I was born deaf. Remember? But I remember the first time I realized there was sound in the world. I was a little girl. Even younger than you are now. I would watch my grandmother—she was hearing—and I noticed, every morning, she would suddenly stop, turn her head, and dash into the kitchen. Why? I couldn't figure it out! So finally I followed her in, and there, on the stove shooting steam into the air, the tea kettle. And I understood... *that* was sound. *(She stops, suddenly struck, continues; remembering as she says it.)* One morning, on the floor, playing with my toys... my grandmother was outside... suddenly I stop, drop my toys, go into the kitchen... something pulls me in... the tea kettle, the steam shooting out... I'm staring at it, but I'm all alone...

*(SLIDE PROJECTION: A child's crayon drawing of a large medical building.)*

*(Dr. Flynt's office. FLYNT sits behind desk. DAN stands near LAURA, who stares off into space. DAN "voices" for LAURA and interprets everything into ASL.)*

DAN *(taps LAURA's shoulder)*. Doctor Flynt is asking you a question. You okay?

LAURA. Yesterday... a talk I had with Adam... *(To FLYNT.)* What was your question?

DAN. Wait! Can we get a professional interpreter in here?

FLYNT. I'm sorry, we don't have an interpreter on staff.

DAN. I thought all medical facilities were required by law to have an interpreter.

FLYNT. All the parents I meet about implants are hearing. If I had known your wife was hearing-impaired, I would have made arrangements.

DAN *(to LAURA)*. I thought I told him.

LAURA *(to DAN)*. You forgot I was deaf?

DAN. I'm sorry. I'll interpret.

LAURA. Okay. But you better say what I sign. *(To FLYNT.)* So, what was your question?

FLYNT. Both your parents are hearing-impaired?

LAURA. No, my parents are deaf.

FLYNT. Ninety percent of deaf people have hearing parents.

LAURA. I know. When I was born deaf, my parents celebrated. 'Specially my father.

DAN. He was going to name you Martha, remember?

LAURA *(cringing)*. Thank God he changed his mind.

FLYNT. My wife's name is Martha.

LAURA. Sorry. It's a lovely name.

DAN *(to FLYNT, explaining)*. Martha for Martha's Vineyard.

LAURA. A mutated gene was passed down from family to family on Martha's Vineyard. Made everybody deaf. Thousands of people. For hundreds of years. So everyone used sign language. Deaf and hearing. People stopped caring who was hearing or deaf.

FLYNT. Then the gene corrected itself. The deaf died out. By 1952 the last one was gone.

LAURA. That's right. The gene corrected itself. God corrected His mistake. Is that what you do with your implants? Correct God's mistakes?

FLYNT. I was taught that God doesn't make mistakes.

LAURA. So was I. Adam's deafness is not a mistake.

FLYNT. Neither is our ability to help him.

DAN *(jumping in).* If Adam gets an implant, how long before he gets his hearing back?

FLYNT. Implants do not restore normal hearing. They do not cure hearing loss.

LAURA. That's right.

FLYNT. You are the first hearing-impaired parent I've had in my office for implant information.

LAURA *(extremely uncomfortable).* I'm trying ... I'm trying to stay open-minded ... as a mother, look at Adam as a separate individual ... not impose my ... not impose my ...

FLYNT. Prejudice?

LAURA. No, my deaf experience.

FLYNT. By that, I mean you are biased. You're his mother. And you're hearing-impaired. How can you be impartial? *(To DAN.)* And how can you?

DAN. No parent is impartial when it comes to their children.

FLYNT. That's why it's important that you both understand what an implant can and cannot do.

*(SLIDE PROJECTION: Child's crayon drawing of the implant, with internal parts labeled.)*

*(Handing them a booklet.)* A cochlear implant uses twenty-four electrodes to deliver sound information to the brain. The implant has two parts: internal and external.

*(SLIDE PROJECTION: Child's crayon drawing of a boy with the area behind his ear shaved.)*

Before surgery, the implant area of your child's head is shaved. A general anesthesia is given. The surgery takes about two hours.

*(SLIDE PROJECTION: Child's crayon drawing of the boy with a large red incision behind the ear.)*

The surgeon makes a large, half-circle incision behind the ear and pulls back the skin to expose the skull.

*(SLIDE PROJECTION: Child's crayon drawing of a surgeon drilling into the boy's skull.)*

The surgeon then drills a small depression into the skull to hold the receiver in place.

*(SLIDE PROJECTION: Child's crayon drawing of surgeon inserting electrodes into the boy's skull.)*

The surgeon then drills a small hole through the skull, into the chamber of the inner ear. He then inserts the electrodes through the hole, into the cochlea.

*(SLIDE PROJECTION: Child's crayon drawing of the boy's incision now sewn up with large stitches.)*

The incision is then closed and the head is bandaged. A small bump will remain behind your child's ear for the rest of his life. It generally takes three to five weeks for the incision to heal.

DAN. And then he can hear?

FLYNT. Not yet. About one month after surgery, your child receives the external parts of the system.

*(SLIDE PROJECTION: Child's crayon drawing of a boy happily wearing the implant.)*

Your child wears the headset behind the ear on the implanted side, much like a hearing aid. Two magnets—one outside, one inside—hold the transmitter in place behind your child's ear. A cord comes down to the speech processor. It translates sound into signals that are transmitted to your child's brain. An audiologist plugs your child's system into a computer. And the twenty-four electrodes are computer programmed specifically to your child.

DAN. Then he hears.

FLYNT. Yes. Then he hears.

LAURA. After getting plugged into a computer.

FLYNT. That's right. *(LAURA stiffens.)*

DAN. So, after Adam is programmed— *(LAURA reacts.)* I mean, once his implant is programmed, he will have his hearing back?

FLYNT. A degree of hearing.

LAURA. How much?

FLYNT. For example, right now Adam wouldn't hear a big jet airplane if it landed right behind him. With the implant, he will hear people talking a few feet away.

DAN. What else will Adam hear?

FLYNT. A phone ring, a doorbell, music. But the world will sound different to him. *(To DAN.)* He'll recognize your voice. But he won't hear what you and I hear.

DAN. What will my voice sound like to him?

FLYNT. Mechanical. Like the voice of a computer. But it will take time for Adam's brain to adapt to receiving sound again. He will need months of work with an audiologist. And a speech-language pathologist. To develop meaningful speech.

LAURA. What about his signing?

FLYNT. The reason for giving him the implant in the first place is to reintroduce him into mainstream life. That includes speaking.

LAURA. What's not "mainstream" about me? I work. I'm a wife. A mother. I vote. I drive. I pay bills. Pay taxes. What part of that isn't "mainstream"?

DAN. You know what he means.

LAURA. I know exactly what he means! *(To FLYNT.)* You don't want him to sign anymore?

FLYNT. There's no reason why Adam can't use the implant, speak and use sign language. It's called "total communication." We want to avoid confusing him.

LAURA. You don't think sticking wires in his head is going to confuse him?

FLYNT. The emphasis of his daily life must be on becoming a—well, not a hearing child, exactly—he'll never be a normal hearing child—

LAURA. Then what is he? A deaf child who hears? A hearing child who's deaf? What is he? A mutant? A machine? A robot with a computer in his skull?

**DAN. He's our *son!* He'll always be our son!**

LAURA *(to FLYNT)*. I teach kids every day. I know what
they want, what they need—

DAN *(to FLYNT)*. She teaches deaf children—

LAURA. Deaf! Hearing! It doesn't matter! Children are
children! Their needs are the same! They need to feel
safe! Belong! Adam will never feel part of the hearing
world because he'll never hear what the other kids hear.
And he'll never feel a part of the deaf world because
he'll no longer be totally deaf! Either way, he'll have
wires and boxes and look like a freak! *(Turning to
DAN.)* And what do you say, when he looks up at you
and asks: "Why, Daddy? Why are you doing this to me?
Is there something wrong with me?" I'd be very inter-
ested to see what you tell him! So you don't confuse
him! What's wrong with being deaf? What do you *say*?

DAN. And what do I say if he looks up at me and says,
"Daddy, you had the chance to get some of my hearing
back and you did nothing!" What do I say then? "Sorry,
sweetheart! It wasn't politically correct"?

*(DAN and LAURA stop. They stare at each other. Both
stunned. A long pause.)*

FLYNT. Well... There's one more piece to the implant that
I haven't told you about.

LAURA. I know! It's an extension cord that plugs him into
the microwave!

DAN *(to FLYNT)*. Sorry. What is it?

FLYNT. You, his parents... You must be in complete
agreement for this to work. And I have to say... these
unresolved issues between you will need to be addressed
before we can proceed. *(Rises.)* Maybe we should stop

here for today. This is a big decision for both of you. We can continue this another time, if you like.

LAURA. I don't think so.

DAN. We'll see. I'll call you.

FLYNT. You need to talk privately. I suggest that you not discuss this with Adam until the two of you are in agreement. If you decide to go ahead, Adam will need more audiological tests and medical examinations. And a psychologist will evaluate both Adam, and you. To ensure that your expectations are realistic. And your motivations clear.

*(He exits. Silence. DAN and LAURA look at each other.)*

DAN. That was like a scene from *The Exorcist*.

LAURA. What do you mean?

DAN. Sometimes interpreting you—for me—is like being possessed. I'm speaking your thoughts, your feelings—out comes all this stuff—I have to say it, feel it— Why did you agree to come here if you hate it so much?

LAURA. Because I love you. Why are you doing this to us?

DAN. Adam is slipping away from me. Out of my world.

LAURA. What happened to *our* world?

DAN. It *is* our world. But with Adam, it's different.

LAURA. Not to me.

DAN. Yes, with Adam, we have to decide—together as parents—what would be best. For him. Not us.

LAURA *(looks at him)*. Best for him. Bad for us.

DAN. We'll cross that bridge—

LAURA. Be careful.

DAN. Why?

LAURA. You may be crossing that bridge alone.

*(They look at each other. LIGHTS FADE TO BLACK.)*

**END OF ACT ONE**

# ACT TWO

*(A SINGLE LIGHT up on PAMELA SCOTT, sitting, facing front. A COURT INTERPRETER stands beside her, translating into ASL.)*

PAMELA *(speaking)*. 4439 Oak Road. We live next door. *(A question.)* My husband and I always thought Dan and Laura were a lovely couple. The four of us would do things together—go out to dinner, see a movie. And whenever we saw a film, Dan would slouch down real low in his seat and secretly interpret the entire movie for Laura, trying not to bother anyone around him. A three-hour film. Isn't that something? *(A question.)* Our son, Mark, and Adam used to play together. Every day. But that stopped. After Adam lost his hearing. It was hard. Mark joined a Little League team with his other friends. But Adam kept coming over after that. For months. By himself. To play with our dog. *(A question.)* No. Dan was very proud of him. He showed me a picture of Adam he always carried in his wallet. It was taken when Adam was two. When he was hearing. In the picture, Adam has his arms spread out, like a bird. Dan said when he took the picture he was playing music on the stereo real loud. And Adam was trying to fly.

*(SLIDE PROJECTION: Adam's crayon drawing of thanksgiving dinner.)*

*(Dining room. The family—DAN, LAURA, ADAM, MAX and SALLY—sit at the dining table. They eat. There is no conversation. After a very long pause:)*

ADAM *(bursting with life)*. HAPPY THANKSGIVING EVERY-BODY!
LAURA *(tenderly to ADAM)*. Happy Thanksgiving.

*(Silence. ADAM pushes aside his plate. Looks at his father.)*

ADAM *(speaking)*. "Dah-Dee"? *(Adults freeze. Stunned. They stare at ADAM. No one moves.)* "Dah-Dee"? *(The adults follow ADAM's gaze to DAN. A very long pause.)*
DAN *(speaking and signing to ADAM)*. Yes? What is it?

*(ADAM points to the mashed potatoes near DAN. DAN passes the bowl of potatoes to ADAM. The adults watch as ADAM looks to his father and smiles.)*

ADAM *(speaking)*. "Dank ... you ... Dah-dee" *(They stare at ADAM, stunned.)*
DAN *(shocked, delighted)*. You're welcome.

*(ADAM looks at them timidly. He pushes his plate away.)*

ADAM *(only signing again)*. I'm full. My tummy explode! Can I play now?

DAN (*only signing*). No. Wait. Every year we sit at the table and tell each other what we're thankful for. (*He looks to the adults.*) Who wants to go first? (*No response.*)

ADAM (*waving arms*). Me! Me! Me! Me!

DAN. Okay ... So, what are you thankful for?

ADAM. I'm thankful for ... Mommy! Best in world! And ... Daddy! And Grandma. And Grandpa. And Batman. And Power Rangers. And Ninja Turtles. And—

DAN. Okay, okay, we get the idea. (*Looks to SALLY.*) What are you thankful for?

SALLY. This year, like all years, I thank the Higher Power for His guidance and love. And I'm thankful for my husband. My daughter. My grandson. (*Looks at DAN.*) And you. (*Very carefully.*) May the voice you hear ... be God's. Not your own.

DAN (*to MAX*). What are you thankful for? (*MAX says nothing.*)

SALLY (*to MAX*). Come on. There must be something that you're thankful for.

MAX. I'm thankful that the Mets traded for a left-hander.

(*The adults force a laugh. DAN looks at LAURA. They stare at each other for a very long time.*)

LAURA. I'm thankful that my son is healthy. And happy. And has a family who loves him. (*DAN waits for more. There is no more.*)

DAN. Is that all you're thankful for?

LAURA. That's all.

DAN. I see. *(No one moves.)* Okay—why don't we clear the table. *(To ADAM.)* You can go play in your room now—

ADAM. You! You!

DAN. What?

ADAM. What about you? You thankful for? *(All eyes are on DAN. He looks at the others. A long pause.)*

DAN. I'm thankful for the gifts Nature gave me. For the ability to think, to reason, to feel, to love. Nothing Nature gives us should be taken for granted... *(He looks right at LAURA.)* Because if we wake up... in the middle of the night... and find that gift is gone... then we are without hope. *(DAN and LAURA stare at each other. The TELEPHONE rings. And rings.)* It's my line. It's ringing. I hear it.

LAURA. So go ahead. Answer it.

*(DAN crosses to his phone. The others remain at the table, silent and unmoving.)*

DAN *(speaking into phone).* Hello? Hi, Mom! How are you? Good... good... No, we just finished... Happy Thanksgiving to you, too. How's the weather in New York? Freezing? *(Brightening.)* Yes!... He's right here!... Hold on!... *(Waving to ADAM.)* It's Nana in New York! She wants to talk to you! Wish you Happy Thanksgiving!

*(He holds out the phone for ADAM to speak into it. ADAM bolts from his chair and runs to the phone.)*

DAN *(to ADAM)*. Speak to her! Use your voice again! You
sounded great! It would make her very happy! Say—
*(Speaking and signing.)* "Hello, Nana! Happy Thanksgiving!" You can do it. *(DAN holds the phone to
ADAM's mouth. The boy signs silently into the receiver.
DAN continues into phone, interpreting ADAM.)* "Hi—
Nana!—Happy Thanksgiving! *(Listens to phone. Then
signs to ADAM.)* She says, "Happy Thanksgiving to you,
too! Did you eat lots of turkey?"

*(At the dining table.)*

MAX. When did that start?

LAURA. I don't know. He hasn't spoken like that in
months.

MAX. Obviously Dan's been teaching him.

SALLY. We don't know that—

MAX. Of course he did! Who else?

LAURA. So? All he said was "Daddy" and "Thank you."
What's the big deal?

MAX. You don't see what Dan's doing?

LAURA. What if Dan's been working with him? Privately.
Adam used to speak all the time! What are you so afraid
of? It's only speech, not cancer!

MAX. First the implant. Now he's teaching our grandson to
speak again.

SALLY. The implant idea was dropped.

MAX *(indicating LAURA)*. Ask her.

SALLY *(to LAURA)*. That was a week ago. I thought it
was over. *(No response.)* He's not still pursuing that implant, is he? Are you?

LAURA. We're still ... trying ... to get things straight between us.

MAX *(fuming)*. You mean you're actually still discussing
that with him?

SALLY. You'd never stick an implant in our grandson—

MAX. You're not even considering it, are you?

LAURA. Shut up! Both of you! Leave me alone!

*(The parents are stunned. They look away from LAURA
as DAN turns front, still on the phone.)*

DAN *(into phone)*. Yes, Mom, he's doing fine ... He's
growing up so fast ... You have no idea ... *(He tenderly
strokes ADAM's head. He looks to the table and speaks
carefully, even though they can't hear him.)* Well,
there's no progress yet, on that issue ... It's still ... very ...
difficult. Maybe someday you'll be able to speak to
Adam on the phone yourself. And he will hear your
voice. Wouldn't that be nice? ... I love you, too. Bye-
bye. *(He hangs up, takes ADAM by the hand and crosses
to the table.)* I'm giving Adam his bath.

LAURA. Fine.

DAN. Does ... anyone want anything?

SALLY. No. Thank you.

MAX. I've had enough! *(Exits, slamming the door.)*

DAN. Okay. I'll go. Give Adam his bath.

LAURA. Fine.

*(DAN exits with ADAM. SALLY looks at LAURA.
LAURA continues; trying to smile.)*

LAURA. Generations of deaf mothers staring at me. *(She rises to clear the table. SALLY stops her.)*

SALLY. Sign is Adam's natural language now. Not speech.

LAURA. I don't know what's natural anymore. Technology makes the impossible possible.

SALLY. That's Dan talking—

LAURA. No, it's me talking.

SALLY. You're changing your mind.

LAURA. I already know your point of view. It's clear. You never go against God or Daddy, so why discuss it?

SALLY. I have my own feelings!

LAURA. You never stand up to Daddy—tell him he's wrong.

SALLY. He's not wrong! Not in this case!

LAURA. Your experience as a deaf woman—and mine— your marriage—and mine are worlds apart. Everything is happening so fast, I just want to grab my son and run!

SALLY. Maybe you should.

LAURA. Dan's still my husband. He's Adam's father.

SALLY. Dan is working against the will of God. Only God knows what's best. For all of us. When we try to force our own personal will against the will of the Higher Power, we fall. Like what Dan is doing now. He's falling.

LAURA. I want to catch him.

SALLY. You will. If it's what God wants. But you must be prepared.

LAURA. For what?

SALLY. God may not want you to catch him. *(LAURA crosses away. SALLY continues.)* I saw this coming months ago. Once Adam stopped speaking. I knew. The more his ears closed the more his eyes opened. His eyes locked onto you, followed your every move. A transformation was taking place. Not in his ears. In his heart. When he looks at you he sees himself. His Deaf Self!

LAURA. But his eyes were confused, too. I was born deaf. I grew up in a deaf family. I teach deaf children. But I had never watched a child—slowly, over time—lose his hearing. Until it happened to my son. I watched this confused cloud pass over his face, as he turned the TV set louder, and LOUDER and still couldn't hear it. He would look at me...his eyes asking, What's wrong with me, Mommy?

SALLY. That's to be expected.

LAURA. I watched his hearing friends make fun of him. They stopped playing with him, went away, and never came back. My little boy's heart was broken. Because he couldn't understand! And the deaf part of me told him, Don't worry, Adam! There is nothing wrong with you! There's a wonderful community out there waiting to love you!

SALLY. That's right.

LAURA. But the mother part of me said, My son is hurting! My son is scared! My son is lonely! And I can't help him!

SALLY. I understand.

LAURA. Well...maybe now I can help him.

SALLY. Remember his birthday party? Deaf children everywhere, happy and jumping like puppies! None hurt, scared or lonely. You're a teacher, find the lesson there. In those happy children.

LAURA. It's not that simple.

SALLY. Yes, it is!

LAURA. Life's more complicated now—all this science, technology—I'm forced to make decisions that you never imagined!

SALLY. I know.

LAURA. We're only one generation apart but it might as well be a thousand years!

SALLY. But one thing never changes! A bond we share so strong, a thousand years ago, today and tomorrow!

LAURA. We're both deaf.

SALLY. No! Stronger! We're both mothers! I'm your mother! True, I never faced computer gizmos or digital wingdings. But I gave birth to a child! That's the miracle. Not these microchips! Remember that! Some things run deeper than science. Are more wondrous than technology. I carried you inside my body and gave you life. Like you did for Adam. It connects him to you and you to me and all of us to a network through eternity more important than any Internet. A woman touches God through the love of her child. You love Adam. You know what's best for him.

*(They look at each other. MAX enters.)*

MAX *(to LAURA)*. You're a grown woman. You make your own choices. When you got married so young, I said nothing.

LAURA. You didn't have to.

MAX. You didn't know each other long.

LAURA. That wasn't what bothered you.

MAX. I said nothing.

LAURA. That's right! The Great Silence.

SALLY. I think all your father's trying to say is—

LAURA. I know what he's trying to say.

MAX. Your marriage is your life. Not mine. But! Now you have a son. A deaf son.

LAURA. He's my *son*, first. Who happens to be deaf.

MAX *(shocked)*. What? That's not what you were taught.

LAURA. Would you have loved me less if I were born hearing? I see hearing parents of deaf children every day in my classroom! They love their children just as much as I do Adam! Deaf or hearing, I'm his mother first!

MAX. You are DEAF first! Adam is not just your life. He's also my grandson!

SALLY. Ours!—

MAX. And we can't just sit and do nothing while your husband pushes an implant into the skull of our grandchild and teaches him to speak behind your back!

LAURA *(very firm)*. Nothing! Do you understand me? Nothing is happening to my son without my permission!

SALLY. Well, we're glad...that's all we...I just can't understand why Dan is still pursuing it—

MAX *(to LAURA)*. —And you're allowing it—

SALLY. Why is he doing this? That's what I don't understand. Why?

LAURA. For Adam's safety. So he'll hear cars coming, or hear someone yelling "Look out!"

MAX. That's not it.

LAURA. Dan thinks more opportunities will be open to him, he can listen to music, improve his learning skills—

MAX. That's not it.

LAURA. Then WHAT IS IT? You tell me!

MAX. Dan thinks we're handicapped. Disabled.

LAURA. No—

MAX. We're people with something missing. Something less than!

LAURA. He doesn't think that!

MAX. Of course he does!

LAURA. No, the truth is, *you* think that! You! About your-self!

SALLY. Let's stop this right now—

LAURA. Dan and I have been married seven years! I'm his wife—not his deaf wife—his wife! He loves me for my heart not my ears!

MAX. I see different.

LAURA. Yeah? What do you see? That he doesn't love me anymore? Is that what you're trying to say?

SALLY. That's not what he's saying

MAX *(to LAURA)*. I see different, that's all.

LAURA. I see different, too! Maybe for the first time! I see how scared you are!

MAX. Scared? Of what?

LAURA. Of Dan! It's a power thing, isn't it? He's a hear-ing man and that terrifies you!

MAX *(exploding)*. Bullshit! That's fucking ridiculous. *(To SALLY.)* Let's get out of here!

*(He crosses away. SALLY follows. LAURA chases after MAX, turns him around.)*

LAURA. That's why you focus on your Deafness—with a capital D! It keeps you separate from the world, makes you different, and you think that gives you power!

MAX. Don't you talk to me like that—

LAURA. The world is Us versus Them! That's why Dan— and my marriage—scares the shit out of you! Because my being deaf was never an issue with Dan, and you don't know what to do with that!

SALLY. THAT'S ENOUGH!

LAURA. You see yourself as a Deaf Man, instead of just as a man!

SALLY. LEAVE HIM ALONE!

LAURA. Let me ask you something. If you suddenly weren't deaf, what would be left of you? Who would you be? You only identify people in terms of deaf and hearing! Even me! Within my own community! Born deaf! Born deaf! As if that made me more deaf!

SALLY *(to MAX)*. Tell her! Tell her!

MAX. No!

SALLY *(to MAX)*. Tell her! Now! The truth!

LAURA. Born deaf! Born deaf! Born deaf!

SALLY *(exploding)*. YOU WEREN'T BORN DEAF!

MAX. NO! *(He tries to physically stop from signing anything more, but:)*

SALLY. You were born hearing! *(Silence.)*

LAURA *(stunned)*. What? *(Silence. LAURA looks to SALLY.)* Is that true? *(SALLY just looks at her.)* Is that true? *(A pause.)*

SALLY. Nine days. I held you nine days. And every minute, of every hour, of every day, I prayed.

LAURA. For what?

SALLY. For God to make you deaf.

LAURA. So I was born hearing...

SALLY. God answered my prayer.

LAURA. And corrected His mistake. Is that what I was? A mistake?

SALLY. God doesn't make mistakes.

LAURA. Then why pray? If you really accept God's will. For nine days you prayed for God to change his plan for me. To impose your will, not His.

SALLY. It wasn't my will. *(Looks to MAX.)*

LAURA *(to MAX)*. Oh. I see.

SALLY *(looks to MAX and LAURA)*. I'm going to wait in the car. *(She starts to exit. Stops. Turns to LAURA.)* You were the most beautiful baby I had ever seen. Perfect in my eyes. To mothers and God, all children are the same. *(She smiles.)* But you know this already. *(To MAX.)* You have five minutes. *(She exits. MAX and LAURA stare at each other.)*

MAX. I walked into your mother's hospital room ... on the day you were born ... and met my little girl for the first time. Your mother held you, wrapped in a pink blanket. Your face was scrunched up, your eyes barely open. Your mother was exhausted, her hair a mess, but she had this glowing smile on her face that I've only seen in some of the religious paintings she's shown me. I walked to the bed, stood behind you, and— *(He claps his hand loud.)* You jumped. And I knew.

LAURA. And you were disappointed.

MAX. Yes.

LAURA. Then what happened?

MAX. I went a little crazy. Said some terrible things. I think I scared your mother. She immediately started praying for us.

LAURA. You don't really believe her praying made me deaf. Do you?

MAX. Your mother can be a very persuasive woman. Doctors told us you would be totally deaf by four or five. **Until then, you'd be severely hard-of-hearing. Without** hearing aids you'd hear very little. Maybe a loud noise. An alarm clock, a siren—

LAURA. —A tea kettle. But you never gave me hearing aids.

MAX. No.

LAURA. You told everyone I was a deaf child. That I was born deaf. Made Mother agree.

MAX. Yes.

LAURA. Why?

MAX. Deaf culture.

LAURA. Because your parents were hearing? I know what they did to you.

MAX. Deaf heritage.

LAURA. Sent you away to that oral institute. They tied your hands so you wouldn't sign. You never saw your family—

MAX. —Very important that deaf heritage be carried forward. Pride. Each deaf generation must hold on to our history, our language, our culture! These implants— where will the technology lead? No more deaf? Wipe us out? Erase us—no, like a computer, *delete* us as a people? These implants are genocide: the systematic annihilation of a people, a cultural group. God wants us deaf! This technology—knowledge without wisdom—we're not smarter than God! Let whatever God does be!

LAURA *(looks at him)*. That's the point. You can't. And neither can Dan. You're the same, really. You both talk of wanting what's normal, what's natural. He's just trying to do to his son what you tried to do with your daughter. Prayer. Microchips. Same target. Different ammunition.

MAX. I only wanted to give you every opportunity as a deaf person. A strong start. Identity. Sense of self. Your deaf self.

LAURA. To teach me who I am, you lied about who I was.

MAX. Yes.

LAURA. And the moral is...?

MAX. Stop. You're being a teacher.

LAURA. I can't help it. It's who I am. And I'm deaf. Maybe not born deaf. But deaf just the same. It's as natural to me as breathing the air. As simple, as basic, and as beautiful as taking a breath. Adam and I are the same. It doesn't matter when we drew our first breath. What matters is that we're breathing.

*(Adam's room. ADAM has had his bath and is now in his pajamas. DAN dries his hair with a towel.)*

ADAM. Did I do something wrong?

DAN *(signing and speaking)*. When?

ADAM. Dinner.

DAN. You did nothing wrong.

ADAM. Everyone stared at me.

DAN. That's because they love you.

ADAM. They were angry at me.

DAN. No. Just surprised.

ADAM. Why?

DAN. You spoke!

ADAM. You angry at me?

DAN. I'm very proud of you.

ADAM *(hands DAN a children's book)*. Read me a story.

DAN *(opens the book)*. There are no pages in this book. What happened to all the pages?

ADAM. Dog ate them.

DAN. We don't have a dog.

ADAM. Dog next door.

DAN. Oh. I see.

ADAM. Read me story.

DAN. There are no pages!

ADAM. Pretend!

DAN. Okay ... This is the story of ... *(Checks the cover.)* Pinocchio. *(Opens the book and mimes turning pages.)* Page one. Once upon a time there was a man. He was very lonely. And what this man wanted—more than anything else in the world—was a son who was a real boy. *(Looks at his own son.)* Instead, he had only a puppet. *(He stops.)*

ADAM. Go on.

DAN. So the lonely man pretended that the puppet was a real boy. But it wasn't the same. What he wanted was a boy who could laugh and sing ... *(He looks at ADAM.)* ... and go to the movies like other kids ... listen to symphonies, hear ball games on the radio, or talk to his dad like a real boy ...

*(Puts the book down and pulls his son close to him. Holds him tight. And doesn't let go. A SINGLE LIGHT UP on SALLY, sitting, facing front.)*

SALLY. I'm nervous. I've never testified in court before. When I was young, the TV show *Perry Mason*—it seemed the lawyers were always yelling at people in the courtroom. There were no captions back then—my parents were hearing, didn't sign—so I never knew what the lawyers were yelling about. I grew up thinking that only people who did bad things were put in courtrooms. To be yelled at by lawyers. *(A comment, unseen by us, is signed to her. She smiles.)* Thank you. *(A question.)* She's an excellent mother. She loves Adam with all her heart. And Dan's an excellent father, too. I remember, one day, he and Adam— *(She is interrupted.)* Oh. Sorry. *(Another question.)* Her ability to be a mother? What do you mean? Because she's deaf? I don't understand what you— *(Another question.)* No, I don't need the interpreter to slow down. The interpreter's fine. It's your question that makes me ... What does Laura's deafness have to do with her ability to be a mother? *(A quick comment.)* No, I'm not being argumentative. *(A question.)* I don't know why she didn't stop Dan right away with the implant! That was a year ago. I've stopped judging that. I'm not going to criticize her as a mother! She was tested!—Do I follow my husband or follow what my heart knows is best for my child? I'm proud of her! Because that's the question, isn't it? What is going to happen to Adam? A year ago, he wiped a painted flower from my cheek. Is that what you want to do with Adam? Erase another flower? Because that's what Adam is! A beautiful deaf flower! He's just of a different color! That all! *(She looks ahead.)* Do you have children? *(A pause.)* I didn't think so.

*(SLIDE PROJECTION: Adam's crayon drawing of an office waiting room.)*

*(Dr. Walters' office. She sits at her desk. DAN bursts in.)*

DAN *(speaking)*. Excuse me, Dr. Walters, the girl outside said to come right in. I've been waiting out there for almost an hour. We had an appointment to see you at three-thirty. To start our psychological evaluation. For the implant. For our son. Well, my wife is late. I called her school. They said she left hours ago. I don't know where she is!

*(DR. WALTERS stops him, and inserts her hearing aid into her ear. She gestures for him to continue. DAN now signs to her.)*

You're deaf. *(WALTERS nods.)* They didn't tell me you were deaf.

DR. WALTERS *(signing)*. Should they?

DAN. Well...yes.

DR. WALTERS. Why?

DAN. Well...I think I should know what—who—I'm dealing with.

DR. WALTERS. Does it make a difference to you that I'm deaf?

DAN. No. Of course not. I just wasn't expecting— I'm a little thrown, that's all.

DR. WALTERS. Why?

DAN. Talking to a deaf therapist—a female deaf therapist—feels, I don't know, unfair.

DR. WALTERS. One partner in this marriage is deaf. I think that's why I was assigned to your case.

DAN. I'm sorry we wasted your time today. *(He starts to exit.)* When I find out what's going on with her, perhaps we can reschedule for another time.

DR. WALTERS. I still have a few minutes.

DAN. What's the point of me—

DR. WALTERS. You're here.

DAN. Yes, I'm here. But I thought the whole idea of this meeting was for you to assess—to psychologically assess Laura and I as a couple.

DR. WALTERS. That's correct.

DAN. Well, I hate to point out the obvious but Laura's not here.

DR. WALTERS. That's correct.

DAN. If she's not here, she can't tell us how she feels about this implant.

DR. WALTERS. I think she *is* telling us how she feels about the implant. *(She looks at him.)* I hate to point out the obvious. *(A pause.)*

DAN. I think I want to leave now.

DR. WALTERS. Okay. *(He doesn't move.)* Would you like a cup of coffee?

DAN. No. Thank you.

DR. WALTERS. Is this typical of Laura? Not showing up for an appointment?

DAN. No.

DR. WALTERS. Why is she doing it now?

DAN. Retaliation.

DR. WALTERS. Against you.

DAN. That's right.

DR. WALTERS. Why?

DAN. The battle lines have been drawn. We need to focus on what's best for Adam! It's got nothing to do with her!

DR. WALTERS. He's her son.

DAN. He's my son, too! No one seems to remember that! Is it a sin to want my son to hear again? Am I now Doctor Frankenstein sticking electrodes in his brain because I want my son to hear music? To go to public schools? To speak on the telephone? To say "No" to a stranger or "Help" when he's in trouble ... and have people understand him? To hear a car coming down the street or his grandma say "I love you"? Is that such a terrible thing?

DR. WALTERS. Of course not.

DAN. Thank you!

DR. WALTERS. But debating the pros and cons of getting an implant doesn't interest me. That's between you and Laura and your physician.

DAN. Oh. Sorry. Am I boring you? Not interesting enough for you?

DR. WALTERS *(smiling)*. No. You I find interesting.

DAN. Well, that's good to know. Maybe I'll stay.

DR. WALTERS. Actually, I have no more time today.

DAN. What do you mean?

DR. WALTERS. Your appointment was an hour ago.

DAN. I know—I told you!—I've been waiting outside! Waiting for Laura! She never showed up!

DR. WALTERS. What can I do? I have a staff meeting in a few minutes. I'm stacked up all day. Like you said, why don't you talk to your wife and reschedule—

DAN. I don't want to talk to my wife! I want to talk to you!

DR. WALTERS. Then let's arrange another time—

DAN. I don't have any more time!

DR. WALTERS *(sincere)*. I don't mean to jerk you around. Really. I'm sorry this happened this way. I would very much like to meet with you again. With your wife. Or you alone. But, unfortunately, now is not the time. If you decide to reschedule, please call me. Anytime.

DAN *(stares at her, goes slowly to the door, stops, turns).* I was sitting out there a long time. By myself.

DR. WALTERS. I know.

DAN. And something occurred to me. Can I ask you a question?

DR. WALTERS. Yes.

DAN. I know the moment when Adam was conceived. Laura and I had just gotten married. We wanted so bad to have a baby. We were on a camping trip. Way up in the mountains. We were hiking in the forest. No one around for miles. She was walking ahead of me on the trail. Leading the way. As always. She had on this blue flannel shirt and shorts cut high on her thighs. We walked off the trail and entered a glade of tall trees, to rest. It was hot. She asked for water. I gave her my bottle. She put it to her mouth. As she drank, the water dripped down her neck, over her chest, soaking her shirt. I pulled her onto a large flat rock. Slid her shorts down her legs. And made love to her. And I knew. I knew we were making our baby.

DR. WALTERS. That's a nice thing to remember.

DAN. No. It's not.

DR. WALTERS. Why?

DAN. Because when I was making love to her...when I was inside her...when I was coming inside her...all I could think about was...my sperm was hearing sperm... And that maybe...maybe... Please, God, let my hearing sperm make us a hearing baby! *(Looks at her.)* Is that bad? *(They stare at each other.)* What time is your staff meeting over?

*(A SINGLE LIGHT on LAURA, sitting, facing front.)*

LAURA *(responding to a question).* I'm a teacher. I teach children. Deaf children. *(Another question.)* I teach them everything. How to count. How to read. How to draw. How to write their name. *(She pauses, thinks, then:)* I teach them that being deaf is something to be celebrated. I teach them not to accept their deafness. Cherish it. Revel in it. I teach them deafness is a blessing, not a disability. That it's a glorious and unique journey through life that offers them a special view of the world that none of their hearing friends will ever know. I teach them to bathe in the beauty of their language, to be proud of their history, their heritage, their culture. I teach them to take the blanket of shame and fear that suffocates them and weave it into a banner of honor. I teach them that their inability to hear has no effect on their ability to think, to achieve, to love. That every day, the sun rises and shines on all of us. Equally. None of us are meant to be sitting in the shade. So I teach the children to stand up. Come out of the shade! Step forward! And stand in the sun! *(A pause.)* I teach them that, because that is what I was taught. By my father. And mother. And now it's my turn. My job. My ... responsibility. *(Beat.)* And that's why I must have custody of my son.

*(SLIDE PROJECTION: Adam's crayon drawing of his **house at night**.)*

*(Dan's study. He sits at the computer. Types. LAURA slowly enters. Watches him. Stands in front of him.)*

LAURA. Adam's sleeping. He asked why Daddy wasn't home for dinner. Or dessert. Or bath time. Or bed. *(He just looks at her.)* I told him Daddy was working late. That's what I told him.

DAN *(signs to her)*. You lied.

LAURA. Yes. I lied.

DAN. That was kind of you.

LAURA. Would you like some dinner? I saved your plate.

DAN. I stayed late at this therapist's office today. Later than I ever imagined I would. Things started to come up.

LAURA. That was fast.

DAN. It was time.

LAURA. What things?

DAN. Hidden things. Buried. For years.

LAURA. Like a virus?

DAN *(looks at her sadly)*. Yes. Like a virus. *(They look away from each other. Then:)* Did you also happen to explain to Adam why Mommy humiliated Daddy today? Why Mommy not only didn't show up for her three-thirty meeting with the therapist and Daddy, but didn't call, didn't let Daddy know she was going to leave Daddy there alone, to get dissected?

LAURA. I'm sorry. I tried to call and—

DAN. And WHAT? You tried and they "didn't have a TTY"? You tried and they "didn't understand how a relay call works"? Bullshit! She was a fucking *deaf* therapist! But you probably knew that, didn't you?

LAURA. No, I didn't know that. And it wouldn't have mattered anyway.

DAN. Oh, is that right?

LAURA. Yes. That's right. Because Adam's not getting an implant. Not now. Not ever.

DAN. He's not.

LAURA. No. That's why I wasn't there at three-thirty. And I did call. I dialed the number. To tell you. To tell you to end all this. And come home. But I stopped. And hung up the phone.

DAN. Why?

LAURA. Because I realized that's not what I wanted. I realized ... that I didn't want you to come home. *(They stare at each other. DAN looks away and begins to type on his keyboard.)*

DAN. There are web sites on the Internet ...

LAURA. I didn't want you to come home. I hung up the phone. My last words were still on display on the TTY: "Can you find my husband for me?" I stared at those words. Because I couldn't find you anymore ... *(She looks at him.)* You've disappeared somewhere! What happened to you? Where did you go? *(No response.)* So I switched off the TTY! Zap! Gone! One plus one makes two, right? I teach math, don't forget! One plus one makes two!

DAN. One plus one ... ?

LAURA. Adam and I.

DAN. Make two?

LAURA. If there's something wrong with Adam, then ... there's something wrong with me. And I don't know when that happened. When did that happen? *(He says nothing.)* Tell me! When did it happen?!

DAN. What?

LAURA. That I became disabled. To you. Dis-abled. Not-able! To what?! Be your wife?! Be your lover?! Carry on a conversation?!

DAN (*speaking only, not signing; his voice exploding from him*). YOU CAN'T HAVE A FUCKING CONVERSATION WITH ANYONE OUT THERE WITHOUT ME! CAN YOU? WITHOUT ME HAVING TO FUCKING INTERPRET EVERY-THING BACK AND FORTH TO YOU! (*He stops himself. Stunned. They both freeze. He resumes signing to her.*) It's not fair what God has done.

LAURA. What has God done?

DAN. He lied. He said my son was hearing and let me fall in love with him. Then I'd see him sitting with you over in the corner, signing away, and I'd think, "No! It's not fair! He was mine!"

LAURA. He was *ours*!

DAN. God gave me a hearing son and then took that son away from me. I want my son back.

LAURA (*looks at him hard*). You can't have him. (*A long pause.*) And then you lied. To yourself. When you said you could still be in love with a deaf woman.

(*They don't move. DAN crosses to the desk. Sits. He begins frantically typing at the computer keyboard.*)

DAN (*desperate*). Maybe it isn't lost. Maybe I can still find it!

(*LAURA lunges at the keyboard and violently claws at it like an animal. DAN tries to fight her off. She rips it from DAN's hands and smashes the keyboard to the floor.*)

LAURA *(exploding)*. WE WERE A FAMILY! *(They stand motionless. The shattered pieces scattered across the floor. Suddenly, LAURA looks offstage.)* I think Adam's awake. Did you hear anything?

DAN. No. I don't hear anything. Anymore.

*(Adam's bedroom. LAURA darts in. ADAM is in his pajamas, looking worried, scared, as if wakened from a bad dream. She scoops him up in her arms and holds him tight. He looks up at her.)*

ADAM. Mommy...?

LAURA. Yes?

ADAM. Am I a real boy?

LAURA. Yes, you're a real boy.

*(She sits, caressing her child in her arms. He closes his eyes. And falls asleep. LIGHTS STAY UP on them as a SINGLE SPOTLIGHT catches DAN, now at the opposite side of the stage—alone, sitting facing front. A COURT INTERPRETER stands beside him, translating as DAN speaks.)*

DAN. Your Honor, a year has passed and I still don't know what crime I committed. What code I violated. But I've been punished. I lost my wife. Please give me my son. *(A question.)* Yes, I am currently employed. I work in an office again. I make a good living. Enough to support custody of my son. I want my son. *(Another question.)* Public relations. Public relations is about perception. How a client wishes the public to perceive them. Who they are, what they do. That is my task. To help them define what it is that makes them unique. Special. That is job. My responsibility. To help them say to the outside world, "I'm different. And I have value." *(He stares front. Tries to smile.)*

*(SLIDE PROJECTION: A sequence of Adam's crayon drawings of the following pictures:*

1.) A COURTROOM, WITH CHILD-DRAWN ARROWS POINTING TO "JUDGE," "MOMMY" AND "DADDY."
2.) FRONT YARD OF HOUSE, WITH "MOMMY," "DADDY" AND "ME" STANDING BY THE CAR. A SUITCASE BY "DADDY." BIG TEARDROPS RAIN DOWN FROM ALL THEIR EYES.
3.) "DADDY" DRIVES AWAY IN THE CAR. "MOMMY" AND "ME" ARE CRYING IN THE FRONT YARD. ON THE DRAWING, IN ADAM'S HANDWRITING, IS SCRAWLED "GOODBYE DADDY.")

*(SLIDE PROJECTION FADES OUT.)*

*(LIGHTS FADE OUT on DAN. LAURA still caresses ADAM in her arms. She kisses her sleeping child and stares out front, uncertain of what the future may hold for them. Then they, too, FADE TO BLACK.)*

### END OF PLAY

# DIRECTOR'S NOTES

# DIRECTOR'S NOTES

# DIRECTOR'S NOTES

.

# DIRECTOR'S NOTES

# DIRECTOR'S NOTES

# DIRECTOR'S NOTES